NICK POWER

CARAVAN

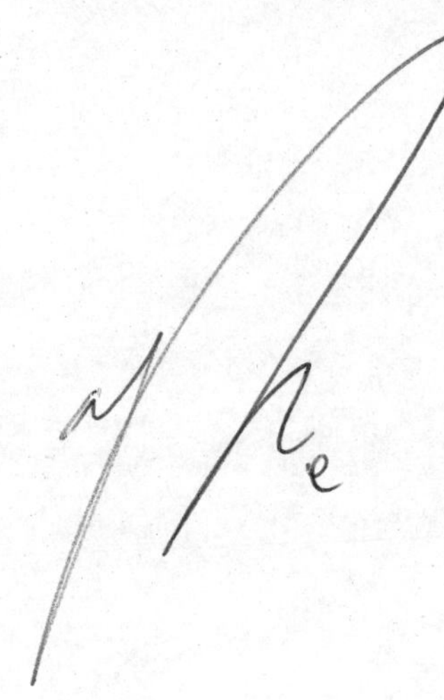

erbacce-press
Liverpool UK

5 Farrell Close, Melling, Liverpool, L31 1BU, UK

Editing, layout and typesetting; Dr. Alan Corkish

erbacce-press publications Liverpool UK 2017

erbacce-press.com
ISBN: 978-1-907878-92-3

Acknowledments:

Sonder magazine, *erbacce* journal, *Coney's Loft* and *Your One Phonecall*

Contents:

Caravan

I saw a gypsy running for
the trees
and all my family, they came out to
see. He had lost his only shelter in
this land

caravan, caravan

I said to him, "where will you go?"
he just laughed and said,
"well I don't know. I'll keep
walking until I find a kennel for my
plans."

caravan, caravan

then he stopped and looked at me
he said, "here boy now do you
think you're free? The sky it holds
my soul
and the rivers are my hands."

caravan, caravan

take me to your greenest hills
out to where the vanished valley
spills
we'll go travelling all across this burning land

caravan, caravan

Inner Narrative

Do not read these poems aloud
they are not for the ears they are
for the eyes
for the inner narrative only
you will not hear them in collapsed
subway tunnels or flooded quarries
you will not hear them in Guinca Gap
Llandudno or Minehead
Butlin's
you will not hear them in reserved
rooms above cafés
or community hall giro schemes
they will not appear at funerals or
war memorials
or anywhere people gather

instead in arcane relapses of the
mind
flashbacks and sequestered
memories
the top decks of buses at dawn
daydreaming thru the page
is where these poems reside

in you
as in me
a remote kind of happiness
exists
for the secret world

Opening

The cormorant there, at the rock's
edge. Enquires the horizon. The
falling sun the silver sea the
wood-rot wharf. Wings dilated,
poised as if to catch the drowsy
aubade

from this sand dune
I see two towns connected by a
static caravan park. Whirligigs whirl
from its barbed fence. Slowly, a girl
drags a tyre across the brush-
scrub, attached by a piece of
electric blue rope

Night Screen Odyssey

They're watching movies again. I hear them from their open bedroom window. Outdoor voices. An opening theme. The screech of car tyres and a high-pitched scream. I'm in a terrace directly beside theirs and every movement, every sound is transparent. I imagine it's what a drive-in-cinema might sound like in 1950's America. But this is North-West England, present day. There are other sounds.

All the films *we* watch seem to be out of sync. The actors mouth words and nothing comes out until seconds later. Explosions are a ball of silent flame. The aftermath nearly rips through the flimsy flat-screen speakers. This one happens as the Monroe lookalike is talking in a room papered with leather-bound books.

Nobody on the screen flinches at the sound of the fireball.

From outside, I hear the wail of an ambulance siren hurtling through the street like some injured bird. I move from the bed to the window and watch it fizz past. I notice the blue light and the siren happen separately from each other; some splicing of the action and the sound. An un-concurrence. The siren warps and distorts the further away it gets, like an old, worn piece of videotape.

She's under the covers now, and I call out to her. I feel my mouth move and half-expect the sound to come seconds later, out-of-sync, like everything in our lives seem to be.

Motocross Drag

After the beachfront fair
they sit

watch men
heave painted scaffold into
vans

argue about
inter-breeding animals
and drug mules

drink and sniff and watch for
movement

there, like hornets under a
gunnysack muffled sun

two scooters burst across the
wet sand
toward the panorama of infinite
Blackpool

each rider dreaming up
the myth of himself

Flyscreen Incident

A touch of the saints he said
crumpling to ground as if hurled
thru windscreen of speeding Corsa
or Astra GTI
severed at the elbows
a touch of the saints it was
it was I heard it
so if I tell you of
people who gave nothing of themselves
mirrored everything I did
then stole it
stashed under static trailers
family I mean
it'd be the hardest thing you'd ever
heard

I'm ok
I can sleep out here
by the box stalls
eat
from discarded nosebags
and someone told me you can also
drink anti-freeze

The Hiding

Trampling down reeds in which to make a cot, she lifts the thing over wooden paling. Sets it prone, backside up. The faint gurgle of spittle-

sh-sh-sh-sh-sh-now

half-sinking in the boggy fescue, she brings a knitted cable snood over its mouth, gentle-like. Wind fusses the saltmarsh like a chorus of whispers. She drags bracken and branches in to disguise the makeshift spoor-

sush now, shhhhh

blanket darkness, rolling hoe-thud of a racing heart, the distant rush and hiss of water converging to a higher point-

well-we-ell-now

she can hear them nearer; hotfooting the damp earth, the braying of radio scanners, nearer, the moist snare of dog's breath in the aestival sweetbreeze, nearer, every stride. She finds its pale face with her hand-

there's-a-ba-ba-there

overhead, the rotary blades of a helicopter come-a-cutting up the sky, then the bright, sweeping accretion of a searchlight. The black beach illuminates like some woven mandala, filled up with pale stars

I Want To

I want to take you from this train
in your stocking feet
and kiss your neck
and not say a word
and not say a word
drive you around cold nightscapes
in stolen vehicles
your eyes willing
flank the new estate and murder
districts
fly along on fumes siphoned from
Texaco tankers
until finally
at the high barn and berm
motion that we may love each other
whistling nothing but air between
our lips

Gloaming

I drive her to work in the early mornings. I'm woken abruptly by a wisp of deodorant that wanders in from the spare room. The cold, perfumed air stings at my nose. I hear her teeth chatter as she sits in front of the stand-up mirror, hums a half-tune that staccatos through her shivering bones. She's easing me up slow-like. At a twenty to seven she'll call my name. Her timing is impeccable.

The newborn sky outside is quicksilver and vast, threatens to engulf our eyes completely. We travel without talking. The long road is bare, save for the odd tractor that will make sharp, unannounced turns into fields of Lucerne and Maize, submit peacefully to deep oceans of golden-green crop. She sits next to me, rigid, willing her eyes open, as if she's still fighting the pull of slumber.

I drop her at the layby cafe and turn around. The smell of fertiliser strong in the brittle air. I drive slowly, scanning the bare landscape as if still in a dream. I pass a rusted car-barn with a painted sign on the door that says BOYS CLUB. At this stage in the journey, my mind is always drawn back to the hungry days of my childhood, when everything in the world seemed infinitely magnified. Crueler, even.

When I was twelve I fractured my right hand on a punch bag in Lingham gym. I sat in the hospital for six hours straight while my parents worked separate night shifts. The big, Hattie Jacques-like nurse called me 'scallywag' and strapped me up in a cotton sling. The touch of her skin made me drowsy.

Behind her, pinned to the high wall, was an x-ray of a woman's body. I hadn't stopped looking at it. It seemed the antithesis to the dull ache in my hand. The smooth curve of her bones and the space between her thighs. Brilliant white light shining through the ghost of her frame. Her name, a scribbled note said, was EMMA RAE. Emma Rae, Emma Rae, Emma Rae.

When the nurse left the room, I slid the radiograph under my t-shirt and held it there with my sling. I seethed away in secret, toward the double-doors of the entrance. I could hear my heart pounding.

In the quiet gloaming, I trudged home, three miles across flooded motorway fields. Upstairs, I tacked the skeleton-image to the dark bedroom window and sat there below it all night, waiting for the sun to come up.

There Are Other Forces

During the month of The Kowloon
I parted ways with my employer
rain degged the raby mere
where misspelled headstones
sprung up
like strangled teeth

during the month of The Golden Wheel
I returned home
a man answered the door
a messianic man at my mother's side
I ran toward Friday's field
a traveller dispute roped me in to its
violent orbit

during the month of The River Queen,
of Town Meadow Supper, a
holy street-war with The Blue Star:
I sequestered myself
frequented lock-ups in Pimbo
played pool with lads I knew
who didn't mind doing time; six
months here, six months there,
whatever
ramraid jobs on juggernauts at

midnight
slinging old Lugers or Colt Navys
straight from a Wild West movie

in the month of The Lobster Pot
I ingested a shiv on Tollemache
Street
convalesced in an old warehouse
for a fortnight
I felt that wild geese and blackbirds
were the makers of a man's fortune
when I crawled out I saw a woman
handing out rail passes
to the overspill build

so I jumped a 508 and raked
macadam for six months
and earned enough to eat
silverside steaks through winter

the month of The Jade Garden
confounded what I already knew:

my life, my fate
are in the hands of other forces

Canicule

Tonight we sleep with all the
windows open
so as to organise our shallow
breathing into
boxcar salvos
that click-clack into
the ether

the Indian summer
embalms us

tomorrow a woman from the council
will knock on the door
and we will lie here
pretend to be dead, deaf
or at imaginary jobs

because we cannot pay her

Fox

Something happened and after I
spent the night under an empty
caravan trying to make sense of it

them that searched for me
searched blind because I am the
only true ranger of this wilderness

a fox in his kingdom of rust an
invisible a stowaway

under the broken boards I laid
things out in front of me
foreign things money a car key
credit cards a Polaroid of three
children in a passport booth

blood-scented so that I belched
and so burrowing into the cool peat

I stayed ’til dawn

I couldn’t face going home
see instead I lay staring at the
flooded pasture thinking of her

oh Shannon remember summer
before you went back to the one-
eyed city that rainy summer?

If She Aches

If she aches into me
I bring in the ache
grind it through the mattress
drown the ache

if she aches an ocean
a river's end an estuary
we put a flame underneath it
smoke out the ache
until the ache withers and dries

if she aches a ritual
a sermon a litany
I cut out its tongue until the ache
is mute
a dumb ache

in the caliginous dawn
by the light of a borrowed
blood-red lamp

we get to working on the ache
while everything here looks
vaguely
Reepherbahn-like

Comedy

If she likes a song she'll listen to it maybe five, six times in a row. Just lie there in bed with the glow of the laptop illuminating her face. The song infinitely revolving, like the old jukeboxes when the needle would jump back.

I wake in the silver break to the chorus of Shack's *Comedy,* a song I haven't heard for near a decade. I'm working away in the next two weeks, almost a hundred miles from here, and she'll be working too, slogging it at the cafe in the stout and devout way she does, gruelling it out for gas money.

All of my possessions are packed inside an army green holdall that stands upright against the bedroom wall. It stares back at me blankly, like some totem of impending solitude. Above that, a hole in the wall is papered over by a faded movie poster: *Bubba Ho-Tep.*

I hear the strummed major chords that bookend the song. Through the top floor window, telegraph wires bob and sway violently with a rising wind. Concurrently, I feel her eyelids blinking against my neck, as if they were synchronised somehow with the electric coils outside.

Trail

Following the trail of her hand

across my body

in the dark

starfish shapes

Catherine Wheel shapes

shapes of perfect geometry

murder shapes

shapes I’m not sure have names yet

First Night Of The Holidays

This is the beginning… the slot-machine zoetrope of pier weekends, of caravan park palladiums, longloping fields of maize and rye that flicker and blink like eyelashes in the dusk, lines of hawser rope coiled around paint-peeled bollards on the wharf. Fishguts rotten in the nose. The stink of life.

Night draws in as we near the gated field. Static houses like sleeping dogs. Everything is connected, everything is new. I dozed on blanketed backseats down miles of Whitsun motorway to be here, to witness this mystery. I slip my shoes off and feel cool grass between my toes. In the near distance, a crowd has gathered at the banks of a canal. A man has waded in up to his waist. He's pushing something up from the water. Another man and a woman grab the thing from his hands, then the man lays it on the grass and presses his mouth against it. The woman is distraught:

"My child"... she's saying... "my baby..."

Something is moving toward where the lights are.

Great Orme

I looked for you
                that year

I looked everywhere

in all the secret places that had
belonged to us
                the year before

Llanddudno
                from top to bottom
was harbouring you

I looked between
all the stationary caravans,
the generators,
the shower blocks

I looked under the
tall chess pieces,
the ballponds,
the coastguard stations
and the cottages

I even looked for your
elephant brother
in the place where
we had
set

the wire trap
between the dead trees
in the rain

but I couldn't see his
lolling angry
head
anywhere

even your father's truck
had left the
patch of yellow grass
exposed

and your mobile was dark
inside

I searched for clues
for a day or more
before I simply forgot
your pale eyes

and my thoughts turned instead
to brown Kestrels
and long creaking piers
that stretched out
to the
horizon

where I first learned to will
the weather
angry

and change the colour
of a rushing river
to bloodred
with just a thought

The Great Orme
   The Menai Straits
         Portmerion
             Llanddudno

they still belong with me

I consider all of them
      to be the sacred
stepping stones of my youth

ones that I
    retrace every
once in a while

only now with a different coloured
ave
 circling
   my crown

Supercasino

I state unequivocally
that I am soaked to the bone
I have been out
darting between cold dunes in the dark
and that
I am tired and alive
and hungry
and that while I may see
all manner of dazzlements
out there
the edgeland
carries its own set of caveats

I will sit here now, and bathe in the brilliance
of an all-night TV gambling channel

Tremarco

He lived in a tent in the woods. He had the tent and the car. That's all he had. You wouldn't have guessed by looking at him. He was always clean, well turned out. He had a pair of jeans and a bomber jacket that made him look like the Red Baron or somebody, some Luftwaffe hot-shot. That was his saving grace I think; people would have abandoned him way before if not for his looks- the hollow eyes, the jet-black cowslicked fringe that stayed put in the wind. Women especially. There were always a couple staying out there with him. Runaways, mostly. He had that kind of magnetism. But he wasn't right somehow. Some glitch in the central wiring, some unbreakable thought-loop. I don't think they knew, the girls. I think they just thought he was *mysterious*.

He'd run into town sometimes. You could hear the drill of the engine. It was a GTI modification job, souped up to four hundred hp. He'd bob into the Shell garage for supplies. The one on the furthest reaches of town, before the bluffs and the dark, leafy valley road. The life would spring back into him in these after-hours interludes. You'd see him at the counter talking football scores with some long distance freight driver. Jaws around a hot Ginsters. Coffee cups on a high table around a TV. The pump-attendants loved him. They'd buy him food. They liked the company I think, on those late shifts. He knew a lot about old movies. He was a good talker. And then just before daylight, he'd return to his spot in the wilderness.

He was searching for something out there. He was hoping to discover a blueprint of some kind, the way craftsmen search for divine secrets in clock mechanisms and snowflakes, patterns of recurring symmetry. Some meaning to his life. He was absorbed in the makeup of ringbarked trees. He'd stand there and stare at them for hours, sometimes well into the night. He'd press his hand into them and wait for a message to come through.

Five-O

Horses in the fading light. Scattered like chess pieces. Staring blankly ahead at who-knows-what. The off-sundial of them stood in the pasture like cracks in a mirror, eyes groping sidewards as if in some kind of trance.

I'm riding a neon green-and-black trial bike that has a defective headlight. Invisible on the road, I'm a death-trap. I'd been scrambling around the dunes up until the wind roused itself into a sandstorm, and so I circled around the brick factory onto the all-night garage road. I stopped here to stare at the horses. That's all.

In the distance, I see the lights of a police car hurtling toward me. As it nears, I realise it isn't police, but a four-wheel coastguard jeep, sea-blue and yellow chequered.

An identical one follows, this time with its sirens whoop-whooping down the coastal avenues. I have to mount the pavement to get clear, as I'm partial to zig-zagging all about the road at this hour, and I'm on the wrong side of the lines.

They're beeping at me as they rattle by, and look to be talking into a radio mouthpiece, so I decide it's time to make myself scarce. I see their tail lights trace against the darkness as they swing a sharp left toward the three-mile concrete slipway. I'm trying to think who'd be stupid enough to be out at sea on a night like this, and then I think back to that lad Rogan and the fishing boat he inherited. He keeps it moored out there. It's where he takes that gang of girls, the ones who're getting knocked backed from the bars every weekend.

Frankie Machine

We spent a whole summer

in that bedroom

clean laundry left to the dew

one night we streamed *Logan*

I ate a plate of steak and potatoes

while you writhed in agony

the ovarian bedsheet curse

by eleven it was still light outside

I pictured myself running again

with the bin dippers

which lit a pilot-light of sorts

and yet the new responsibility I had

tore that picture from my mind

extinguished the flame

me in the sunken armchair next to you

I felt we were bound forever

like Frankie Machine and Zosch

When K Left

When K left the compound
sky hurtling down under
weight of itself
the outline of her gait
down Kirkmaiden
with bags
slowly I began seeing her
in things left behind

going into flights about objects
she seemed to inhabit
colours too
you might have spotted me
in the wetland
digging
I imagined her jewellery as seeds,
for planting

Back To The Old House

Sifting through her grandmother's things. Bags of photographs with chipped frames. Russian dolls and Frozen Charlottes. Pewter tankards inscribed with good luck messages. Football trophies in tall glass cabinets. Liquor. Marble bookends. A huge Yamaha organ with speaker and foot pedals. Brown and lime green carpet underneath reclining leather couches. A brass urn looks out at a sickle of bungalows. Wood panels everywhere. The remnants of life.

She'll come downstairs in an array of dresses, pristine fabric dresses from the fifties and sixties and say, "are you sure you're not bored? You should come up and look at these, there's money in some of the pockets."

Nothing Will Wake Me

Nothing will wake me not even the
shift of the earth
nothing not even the graze of a
knuckleduster or a Gerber knife
not even shingles
or death's reckoning will cause me
to stir

when they come
that will be me up there on the
marble grandstand
conducting the pole-dancers
who are also asleep and dreaming

Wimbrick Hay Orphans

Wimbrick Hay orphans
Kilgarth brawlers
St Benedict's young offenders
Victoria Colts
suicide kids in this area

where has the moon gone?
who made the sky an infinite
bodybag?
where are the cadavers of missing
swans?
who dug out the guts of our war
heroes
like strawberry punnets?
who has hijacked the hourglass of time?

social workers have been searching

the night for you
in vain

they bed down now
mend fist-holes in fibreglass walls
sing lullabies to cheap wooden
elephants
below glow-in-the-dark
constellation stickers

that splay across the ceiling of
empty
twelve-bunk bedrooms

and you, you are somewhere else;
out there
playing kerbie with a glowing
satellite

Dog Thieves

He tested me as we walked through the dark kennels me at his heel like one a the dogs we'd broke in to steal. Some of the kennels had small lights on in them and you could see the dogs bunched in together like tinned fish. Some of them were crying and some of them stared straight ahead just like painted toys. One or two would bark from time to time and he'd dip a bony finger into the breastpocket of his Stockman duster and toss a Jumbone or a Fish Skin to the side of him and the sound of barking would be replaced by the scurrying of feet and lapping of tongues. God knows who he'd paid off to get the electronic punch-code that parted the barbed gates but he'd needed only one shot. The sign on the gate said SEACOMBE but when the gate split so did the words and I pictured a hairbrush made from a shell.

I wondered where Leon and Raelle would be around that time in the night. I imagined them in the shed with the Xbox on and the sleeping bags across the settees, the lava lamp and ripped posters hanging from the woodchip. I wished I was a part of that picture. He pointed as he walked,

"What dogs are them?"
"Irish Setters."
"Irish Setters what."
"Irish Setters Mr Hibbs."
"An' what makes em diffrent from a Inglish setter now."
"The redness in the coat Mr Hibbs."
"Correct."

We ventured around a huge circular Koi Carp holding tank and everything smelled of guts and sex suddenly, and then it began to spit, sparse, heavy droplets of rain as big as your fist and one hung off my nose before I wiped it.

We stalked toward the back fence to a larger paddock with the roofing felt ripped off and silver flashing tape desperately attempting to conjoin the wall and the broken roof. It sagged and lagged with the converging rain and the flimsy wall rocked.

We stopped outside the large pen which looked to be empty through the diamond-wire grill. It were secure though Hibbs had to bring lock cutters out of his long jacket and stood there wrestling it until there was a gentle snap and the pen door swung to.

Hibbs moved toward a corner where I could see a smudged ball of white I knew it was a dog. It was on its back legs about to saltate, body arched like a halfmoon. He was whispering to it and it were purring back at him and then Hibbs quick as a flash was stood over the thing, and he called me in then.

Hibbs was crouched on top of the dog at its croupe, his knees penning the hindlegs in. I could see then that it were a Bullterrier white as a ghost with the long muscular mouths and pink albino eyes like a killer's eyes. Hibbs said,

“Go in this pocket”

I reached over and dipped into the pocket and brought out a fountain pen. I held it up.

“That’s to go directly up its hoop if its jaws lock aroun me arm. Ony way to break it”

“Alright.”

Hibbs had the thing grabbed by the dewlaps and its nose forced skyward. It thrashed its muscular neck from side to side but Hibbs were whispering in one of those erect ears of his and it settled then and I was able to clasp the linkchain lead together just below the grizzle of bone called the occiput. My god the thing was enormous, fists of muscle jutting out of every limb. Hibbs pushed me away gently, took the lead from me and released the jaws of the dog. It were very placid and obedient from then because Hibbs has a way with dogs.

I trailed him as I had on the way in, the path become a muddy sedge, the Bullterrier on the lead navigating puddles and rimples with ease I swear the thing was so white it could only have come from the afterlife.

Partway through our egress from the pound, Hibbs stopped dead on the path. He looked sidewards the Bull at his heel and the patty-pat of rain around the rim of his hat were all I could hear. His crooked bulbous nose silhouetted like a hand puppet. He moved toward this cage that was part hidden by a dirty bathtub n crouched down.

Inside was a black Lab that had bit through the wiring, I saw it were lying in its own piss and shit, whimpering. It shivered like the way a drunkard shakes in the sun. One if its paws had gone clean through a piece of barbed wire so Hibbs lifted it up and cut the piece of wire with a butterfly knife and eased the wire through the dew claw releasing a whinny of blood. The Lab whimpered I felt a lump swell in the back of my throat.

Hibbs picked it up, hoisted it with his forearms and balanced it sidewards at his breast. The Lab didn't fuss at all I'm guessing because life couldn't get any worse for the poor sod.

Hibbs turned to me n I swear it's the only time he ever looked me square in the face. I'm not sure if there were a tear in his eye but I wouldn't bet on it.

"Let them all free" he said, and turned, walking with the Lab in his arms and the Bullterrier trailing, toward his truck.

I went back into the compound and ran unlatching all of the cage doors it was such a sight. The dogs you couldn't see them for dust every one bolted past me and down the track past Hibbs and a huge rusted satellite dish that were encumbered with weeds and roots, and then the dogs they were gone into the black beyond.

You could hear them whooping and barking over the wet hummocks as the truck growled away they were like manic jailbirds cursing through a midnight brothel.

Yard Yarn

We sit in the yard
sip at Glen's
listen to Blossoms and Easter
Everywhere

evening falls
the outer world hisses like a taped-
over cassette

strained sounds: sirenwails and
squawks are at once sharp and
truculent

we are enclosed

you say:
"this ring you bought me has
turned my finger green."

I poke a stick into a smoulder of
ashes

laughing, you ask to paint my
toenails

I shake my head, spit

later the red bath roars
your four year old nephew staring
at your bits as you undress

in the grey dawn I wake on damp
concrete

cuticles of one foot the colour of
B-movie blood

Every Wounded Soul

Every wounded soul

all the pulled-apart nerves

and knotted guts

hearts that are heavy as a hundred-ton

feelings that coalesce in some

boiler-room immersion tank

of the spirit

I sense them all I receive their

marking of time   I endure their

counsel

I wait on abandoned platforms for trains

work jobs that pay in wads of

grubby notes

beyond a bottlegreen signalpost

there   pushing into open sky

a bird with black and white plumage

glides across the salt marsh

City-Stopover

Protein guzzlers spacewalk the
pavement   modified engines
purr thru   illicit thoroughfares
in mock laughter   the sun has
been   six days   sectioned
we're navigating   a star   path thru
midnight   flesh   pots

under the neon moon:
I'm frightened as a deer
I long for the suburbs
I want to light a fire in the woods
I'm wrestling a wired jaw
I have a knife somehow
I have no bed

and
Jodie   Jodie   JODIE HANG ON
Jodie HANG ON   A SEC sprinting
on the balls o' my feet across
cobbles   I'm an apparition
I'm invisible   I'm sure
I'm sure   I am

The Man In The Next Room

Neighbour, in the forestfire of July

in the humid bankholiday on our
street
where unfurnished new-build
houses
observe us, mute-faced
in the macadam melting sun

neighbour, I can hear you
I can hear your footsteps thunder
across the hardwood like
hooves

I smell your tyre-pyre in the night-reeking yard

I hear your divinings, your digestion tract
your parasites

and the psychic thrum of your
pregnant girlfriend

heaving herself up the staircase

even the ambulance taking her screaming
into the twilight

neighbour, who will hide your snide
parcels while you're in the drunk-
tank?
who will defend the beds of those
children?
who will extinguish the chip-pan
inferno as you peg for bail?

I will, me   the man in the next room

because I am the only one left

and I wish you'd let me sleep
just for one minute, neighbour

I wish you'd let me sleep

Blessings For The New Born Baby

Let it be known to everybody in this road

let it be known

this child is sacred this child is protected

let him walk freely between cracks in the pavement

let him whistle the evening in without fear

let him not suffocate in fly-tipped refrigerators

or bonfire sarcophagi

let him not dream in aerosol technicolor

but in wild greens and the sapphire

of the sky

let him not stray into the arms of avenue-purring Ford Capris

or imitation policemen

let it be known

that this child has the eyes of the world upon him

Wearing My White Shoes In

Just thinking on how long I could go without movies through a winter like this one. See, in the January slump is where the real challenge lies. I can go days wrapped in a quilt, as if wearing some plucked ermine, bathing in nothing but the warm glow of the TV.

It's three days after Christmas and I'm walking up and down this vague trail of tarmac wearing my white shoes in. Trying to accumulate some natural scuffs or stains or sign of use.

They're too white, see. The brilliance of the leather has made me uneasy.

Stucco

We eat meals in beachfront show homes. Buildings that lie dormant for months on end. Pristine bungalows and Greek-style stucco villas that spill onto chalk white cliffs and lead to the sea. We watch them for days to make sure they're empty. They're always empty.

We see people from time to time. Professional types in three-piece suits, struggling to open double doors with weighty keychains. They're flanked usually by nondescript families who dawdle nonchalantly about the grounds, bored by their own middling success. They never return. Nobody wants to live here.

Under the cover of darkness we creep in with bags of Chinese takeaway and stack them on huge maple wood dining tables. We light candles, tip metallic cartons of steam and rice, deep-fried fish, dumplings and noodles onto immaculate china plates. Beef Satay and plum sauce. Prawn crackers.

We blow thin layers of dust from blunt cutlery and eat and drink in silence, and somebody laughs and brings a birthday cake out like they do in the quayside restaurants.

The effervescent fizz of sparkler-light reflecting off newly painted skirting boards.

The one we've invaded tonight has a hearth, and an artificial mantle piece. A digital loop of a burning log fire dances endlessly on a screen. Most of us here do this frequently, but there are always new people who come. A black kid who's had his boxing license revoked for fighting in a bar. Spotty mouthed glue-sniffing twins. A girl who says she was interviewed for *Babecast* before they found out her real age. Bored kids from the rich end of town looking for kicks.

At the end of the night, we ransack the place. We spit blood into the carpets. Fuck in duck-down duvets on king sized beds. Shit in polished enamel toilet basins and piss in the bath like corpses. We lie there and pretend we're dead in the stink of ourselves. We write messages on the gleaming tile-sheen: HELL HERE.

We restore some life into those sanitised ghost-condos, because we need, in some way, to let somebody know that we exist, that we're alive. And then we leave.

Depth-Charge

She'd take sick animals in off the street. Birds, dogs, whatever. Injured or lame animals. Hungry animals. Animals that had gone stray or had been dumped on waste ground, left for dead. There were pallet cages in rows all through her back yard and the faint scratch of life at the end of a dangling thread.

There was even a swan that had a burnt mass of bubble-shaped skin growing from its neck, and it would lie there still, coiled and blinking.

She housed the animals herself because she hated the RSPCA and wrote them furious letters all the time. She never said why.

Once, out of the blue, she told me she had been involved in forging bank notes. Around the mid-seventies. She explained it was a complex process that involved sourcing different components of a printing machine in countries across Europe. Switzerland, Germany, Poland. You had to buy the different parts and then have it assembled in a safe house somewhere. It was the water mark that was most important.

I'd do small jobs for her in the yard, cleaning jobs mostly, because the smell of the animals would get into the neighbouring houses and people didn't like it. But I liked her, and I wanted to keep the peace. And besides, she'd pay me handsomely in exotic booze, Polish vodka with huge brown herbs floating inside. Rocket fuel.

It was when we were sharing a bottle she revealed that as a child, her father had made her drink fluorescent paint, the thick emulsion stuff that stinks, and she'd never got rid of the taste from her mouth. She found this funny somehow. And when she laughed the bones of her face would light up, glow-worm like, as if someone had shot a depth-charge to her arse.

So That The Road Rides Even

So that the road rides even
even as spirit levels even
even as supermarket carpark even
even as green snooker hall baize even
even as suicide suspension bridges even
even as floor beneath the penny pushers even
even as a barstool even

then we may have to
work the night in
shifts
clear the incline of
bollards
fill divots in with putty from the
frames of derelict warehouses
send flares into the sky
above your town
so that the road rides even

Chupa-Chups

Saturday night in the cinema

on my own
again

watching *Nocturnal Animals*

later, I'll prowl
the labyrinth avenues
aquaplane through drainage
ditches
and car-ponds
watch distant bars I've been barred
from

wondering where my place is in all
of this

Remote Viewing

Blood chant and the fireplace
The Hills Have Eyes from a wall
mounted set
movie marathons thru cold
afternoons
it's all we can do to keep afloat

while it rains
we play albums with black sleeves:
Halcyon Digest Tonight's the Night
Jack Orion   Sabbath4   Bleach

If I had the presence of mind to flog
the Gibson
we'd be two grand in the green
and out of this mess

but some proclivity to roost in the
mire
prevents us

mornings with vague strangers

waking up on dirty settees of the
soul
and expecting to be saved

O God

O God it happened
we'd been runagates once
street wanderers
attuned only to laughter maps
and dead-ends

siphoning wi-fi from lowlit terrace
alleyways
the pop of faraway exhausts
our work alarm

I think about the fire

in the preliminary months
we'd lived with
a joyous
abandonment

Blarney Stone lock-ins
the wet trees at night   sex in
graveyards

Weigh The Weight

Weigh the weight of....
weigh the weight of love
weigh the weight of heartbreak
weigh the weight of bloodshed
of failure at its
cruellest
the journeyman boxer in cold
shower after taking a fall
in the fifth
weighing the weight of regret

weigh the weight of....
weigh the weight of dreams
weigh the weight of gut-bursting desire
lying atop summer quilt three a.m.
police scanner squealing about
the room
n wanting to vault thru the window
to run with criminals down

wet unnamed streets
weighing the weight of freedom

weigh the weight of....
weigh the weight of anguish
weigh the weight of chance
confessing love in the backroom of
a brewery tap
n later, thieving from the tills
a chase spills out into the mad
night
caught cold by an axe handle
the back of my head in a gutter
chunks of skull missing
weighing the weight of the human soul

a feeling of warmth then:

all the stray dogs pour from
alleyways to receive me

I am alive here

Happy Ending

I'm sat in the car park waiting for her to finish up at the gym, headlights firing bright beams against the concrete leisure centre wall. There is an exercise class in a high room above the entrance, a huge, long windowed room that I recognise as the same room I got a concussion in aged seven, when a Judo instructor somersaulted from a trampoline and landed on me, sandwiching my skull between him and the hardwood floor. I spent two weeks in hospital.

I find I'm running my fingers down a scar at the back of my head when I'm jolted back into reality by a man shouting at his son. The kid is limping, tears streaming down his face. He's dressed in a full Barcelona football kit. They're walking toward the indoor five-a-side courts and the kid looks to be in some pain. "Run it off", the man keeps repeating, hot at the kid's heels. They disappear beyond revolving doors into the bright reception. A huge, high painted sign proclaims SPORT FOR ALL.

Upstairs, the people in the exercise class are engaged in some interesting routines. They begin by bouncing up and down with their index fingers extended at the back of their heads like bunny ears. After that, they pair off and sit opposite one another with the soles of their feet touching. There's a man in the corner of the room with a djembe strapped around his neck. He hits the drum periodically, which seems to signal the end of a particular exercise. Everybody segways into the next routine as if telepathically. I can't make out whether it's an aerobics class or some sort of avant-garde theatre group. Everybody in there is laughing hysterically, looking out to where I'm sat. I'm not entirely sure they can see me.

Man

A man in front of me
keeps stopping
to study trees
to study missing posters
to study bugs
& brickwork
as if there were nothing better to do

I want to kill that man

I want to box him with bees' nests
around both of my fists

this morning I woke up on the bathroom floor
saw lots of faces
in my mind

I thought I'd forgotten existed

strange
seems like
I'm always looking
for the next book
or the next film
or the next pome
that might save me

some great redeemer

this week it's going to be The Bible
after that I don't know-
How To Hypnotise People
or similar garbage

Circuitry

I'd like to be less aware
of the circuitry
of the soul

walk in the house
every once in a while
stretch out my arms
and yawn
announce an early night
fall asleep in the dark room
to muffle of TV voices
through the floorboards

and sleep is plentiful & enough
I am not stirred
by greed or thirst or the fantasy of
greatness

I am good

Billy Big Balls

I strutted around that day
like Billy big balls
laughing in the face
of friends   of enemies
prouder than a pea-comb
until I found out it wasn't
really me   she'd mentioned
on local radio   it was a
different Nick   this one
lived out past the bluffs
where the mansions are
he tended horses ran cars
and   boxed   for the county

Straight To DVD

We're going straight to DVD. Into the bargain rack, suffocated in colourful labels and special offer stickers. Months in a basement storeroom, waiting to be rescued by the Sunday supplement free giveaway. Providing all goes to plan, that is.

We mooch about industrial estates until we have some semblance of a script. Round and around. The body sprayers. The timber yard. The circuit gym. Every sad building corrugated and faceless. Sometimes our characters don't speak and sometimes they do. We'll spend hours on a plot twist. Back and forth until we're satisfied that the thing can be worked into a screenplay. People approach us and pitch ideas:

"I keep having dreams that my shoes don't fit", a man in a dirty blue jumpsuit offers, "that the heels have collapsed. The arches have gone flat. In the dream I end up burning the shoes on a scrap pyre but they refuse to ignite. Instead they sit there staring back at me and turn the colour of crude oil."

They're not always this coherent; some ideas we have to dismiss on the spot, which doesn't always go down well. Everyone around here wants an input, a slice of the action.

We'll convene later in the evening at a bar somewhere, etch the outlines of a thread on the back of old bills or beer mats. Hang scuffed skin over a frail skeleton. When it feels complete we hand out scripts to everyone at the lock-in, head down to the jetty and run the thing through, scene by scene. There'll be a high wind and some emptying of guts. Bottle caps popping. We wrap and return to the snug in the bright morning. This is how we work.

Days later we'll send large brown-wrapped parcels out to all the big studios. Wait at the gates of huge mansions and shove them through the windows of cars that belong to our beloved soap stars. Documents that we're not sure ever get read.

We're certain of one thing though: whatever happens to our film, there'll be no cinematic release. We're going straight to DVD. It's the best we can hope for.

Draw

I’m drawn constantly
to those rare moments of relief
an exhale
simple breath
asleep in the summer field
fire eking out its last filament of light
wild dogs running to horizon
I turn to her
n see a lifetime sear by
as marbled meat burning
on brick
8mm spool of film
in projection room
flashing
feel instantly
that love may conquer
if not whole darkness
then a scuffle or two
at least

Afterward

After searing heat
I walk in the rain
toward Squibb & Cadbury's
find myself facing
huge fibreglass Concorde
replica
commemoration of England's
engineering prowess
weeds jut out of the concrete
around it
remains of a bonfire wearing a
chemical bin
huge dead factory weeping
like some 70's TV celebrity,
bankrupt

lad in green golf visor & oversized
jumpsuit
rakes the vestige:
"Do you know the boys from the
Red Triangle?" I ask. "Mike Scorah
and that?"
"I am Mike Scorah," he says

Tasha

Tasha walks the morning out
bleaches our porches w/
bucket & brush
flip-flopping the marl

her mobile is a hermitage;
distant relatives, siblings
who drafted themselves to war
are sad shapes etched
into eyes
as pareidolia

I always thank her
before she leaves
continuing her rounds

"family's family" is the thing she always says

Field

Burnt field blood field, smell of horseshit-mud field,
houses backing onto fields lead-further-out-to-more
fields, junk field corpse field, I've-just-found-a-scythe
field, tyre field quiet field, forklift-on-fire field

nothing out here but fields, fields, fields

grass and charred scrub field, silence-is-building field,
population none field, everybody gone field, owl field
night field, constellation bright field, soft-hard-soil
field, procession in the toil field, no telephone field,
out here on my own field, army shooting range field,
abandoned in the rain field

nothing in my mind but fields, fields, fields

dog walking night field, rope hanging high field, noose
swinging loose field hanging from the tree-

endless flat silent fields and nobody to walk in them
                but me

I Saw The Burry Man

I saw the Burry Man

in his clean overcoat of Spring

surrounded in green   moss-bearded

burrs and ferns and flowers

sipping whiskey from a straw

I stood with

the crowd as he walked blindly

aided by men we recognised

the priest from Our Lady of Pity

standing kerbside shaking his

hairpiece his adamsapple but

the Burry Man brushed him aside

and everybody laughed

he went on til sundown

all across town

dark spirits cowered in his wake

like mange cats

I slept well that night

Scanner

'Once we sat up in the back of a grockle shell with a police scanner that belonged to the dad of a girl I knew. Her dad was a HGV driver and the static lay at the back of a field by a stretch of dirt that was then used as a construction access road. There was also a car pond there.

Inside there wasn't much by way of furniture save for the bed and bedsheets and a couple of chairs but there was an old Singer all black and gold-painted how they used to be. Outside in the grass a ceramic bath with a tiny rabbit's skull in it along with one white Reebok boot, pancaked and sun-parched, splayed flat like a long yellow tongue.

Yeah we'd sit there in the cold afternoons mostly her opposite me on the bed with the huge

CB Radio between her palms and I'd put my coat on backwards, knees tight against my chest and sit there like a mollusc listening to police activity. Nothing much ever happened. I think we expected there to be more bloodshed or flash of danger at least. She'd cartwheel up and down the dinette after the batteries ran and we'd have to leave before the night descended fully or we'd be sitting there in the pitch dark.

One time we dragged a huge suitcase down from on top of a cupboard and she climbed inside, the frail skeleton of herself so that she became snail-shaped. She didn't stop giggling even when we closed the lid and carried her all the way to the Bus depot and just left her there. Security thought it was a dead body until she jumped up and darted away all of us in stitches. Ian Murgatroyd filmed it on his phone.'

Eviction Night

Recent animals
shards of bone in the
wet cut
jaw of a mountain range
coruscates
crushed tinnies
& smouldering butts
smoked down to the
letters

war things!

outside
our biggest man goes around the site

addressing people
w/ his finger:
y'hear me?
y'hear me?
we don't fucken budge y'hear me?

I nod when he speaks

over his head
Gulf Oil sign
brings to flashing life

as if it were the eve of
death's debut

Pull Toward The Refinery

Hungry days of break-ups
and beer-fights

she-loves-she-hates-she-loves-
she-hates me

"I just thought you were a bit more
put together than this."

fervoured arguments
next to
brass Budweiser tanks
in burger bar foyers

ghost bicycles tied to Christmas
lampposts
offer psycho-comedy
escape

the year races to its inevitable and violent
end

Slip Road

in Leasowe the small

night dances in as delicate as

carrion wings

the slip road beach

gives pale children

ghosting to and fro

on hoverboards

glowing ultra violet

like futuristic

mermaid-holograms

Banging On

The day

is perfect   still

blue-tuxedo-bingo-sky

the rustle of tarp

wind chimes

nearby

aeroplane

dawdles above

us

perfect plumes of contrail

dissolve

in its wake

right on cue

from next door’s yard

Sherley starts banging on

about

the shadow government

Lacuna

To exist where aestivation
meets the Cala-Gran:
I am grateful
I am grateful for the time-keepers
of England
& their gift of light

I am also grateful for a bed

to lie beside the outline of a body
no matter how unfamiliar
a godsend
I am grateful for sleep
thru long evenings

in dim bedrooms I imagine doors
being kicked open

& note all
avenues of escape

And That Dream Again

And that dream again
I'm with the band
top deck of
depot bus we're smoking Embassy
sarcophagus of palmhouse
post-inferno
blurring by

backseat and Hispanic girl
not my wife
I the cuckold
BBC wristbands for some show or other
I worm into her
old man with mouth missing
darts the aisle toward me
carrier bag of glowing
teeth

I jolt awake & confess the whole thing

see what you get
she says
see what you get when you cheat on me
even in your mind

Dead Rubber

Thanks for letting me win
no honestly
I wouldn’t of
I wouldn’t have stood a....

side by side
we survey the morning
a copse of trees
suddenly skirted
by fog
one of my knuckles bleeds

later I walk through town
with the rehearsed gait of a victor
unconcerned with the truth

some people record me

**The Doomsday Clock Moves
Three Minutes To Midnight**

O men of education and potruding
adamsapple
women of law and business ledgers
scientists atomic engineers warfare
tacticians
military accountants people of god
armsdealers

hear this:

I have knotted nooses
unpicked handcuffs
broken the necks of tiny birds
and braised them on bonfires
for food
slept rough on anti-homeless
stalactite spikes
outside the Bank of England
on Castle Street

incarcerated   I read that
Nicola Tesla electrocuted an
elephant
in the name of science

ate three meals a day

liberated myself into a street of
sleet
and oil drums   bailiff clamps

babies borned in burned-out
Cosworths

not a single one of you
know a thing
of
my wars

Morning Eyes

Your black eyes

in the morning

marble eyes

ancient granite eyes

doll eyes

of a doll

for three seconds or so

you are not entirely

sure

if it's me

Our Red River

Come back
come to the surface
won't you?
I love you more than sleep loves you
more than the deep peat loves you
more than the wind turbines love you
more than the monotonous
promise of pharmaceuticals
love you
the knife-patterned ceiling and its
kaleidoscope nightmare
I'll confess I've seen it too

come back
from the fathoms
of our red river
the magnified clockwork
of its fingers
that beckon you in
some ha-ha pendulum

constant

like-this-like-that

Gaff

the man prepared food   for us
while we waited   respectfully
mute on a peach settee
his farmhouse smelled of canola

he mixed eggs in a cut glass bowl
you pulling at your skirt hem   me
extending my foot then retracting
as if in   hospital waiting room

he said he knew a good mechanic
and while he worked maybe he & I
could gaff for a   fish or two
in his stream   to which I nodded

we ate on a huge refectory table
he talked strange & constantly
n when he went for wine you
looked at me & we bailed sudden

we simply abandoned the car
n walked the twenty four miles
home skirting theM62 past a
sculpture they call The Dream

it took us a complete & beautiful
sixteen hours you said you didn't
see your daughter the whole time
not once in any cloud pattern

Love Has Closed For Winter

The man on the bridleway with the stirrups dangling and the frayed saddle over one shoulder, he knows that love has closed for winter. And the night watchman in the Amac Concrete yard, he's aware of it, too. The kids behind the frosted glass of the old lifeguard cabin huddled together drinking Robitussin from the bottle, they know that love has closed for winter. And all the waltzer operators on the palsied adventure lot stare at frosted guard rails and know that the seasons are immiscible. They've realised along with everyone else. Somehow the great fissure of this town, surrounded on one side by the sea and on the other by loping, barren fields, knows in the very fabric of its being that love has closed for winter. And that the summer itself is looked upon as some great comforter, some holy Paraclete. And then even the pylons and radio relay towers, incapable of emitting any discernible phone signal, they know. It's carved into the pillars of the pavilion. Into the sad oddity museums and electronic repair shop yards, piled high with old keyboards and cracked monitors. Circuit boards like splayed veins in mossy divots. The billboards might proclaim it, but everybody knows already. They don't need telling that love has closed for winter, and that they're stuck here, stuck like wasps in a jam jar.

And No Light Shall Falter

I will make you a pallet-bed
cardboard and eiderdown
for your return
I will allay joint pain with diazepam
scored from a man in a clamping yard
I will lurk about the hospital until
you are released

when you are free
I will run between the gables of every building
illuminating them with fire
part rainclouds with roped
ploughblades
to let the new sun through

I will bring a thousand beams to your dulled eyes
and no light shall falter
and no light shall falter